From. The L G
..........................1938
To M B R
for Mrs Wilson

ORDER 85

Please Supply the undermentioned Goods:—
An Invoice or Delivery Note with above Order Number must Accompany the Goods)

1½ yds Linen. T·S
Red IRH. Guinea X
Like pattern sta

Signature...... M Rose

Jane Weir

Walking the Block

Templar Poetry

First Published 2008 by Templar Poetry

Fenelon House,
Kingsbridge Terrace,
58 Dale Road, Matlock, Derbyshire
DE4 3NB

www.templarpoetry.co.uk

ISBN 978-1-906285-19-7

Copyright © Jane Weir 2008

Jane Weir has asserted her right to be identified
as the author of this work in accordance
with the Copyright, Designs and Patents Act 1988.

Images and Pictures ©
Crafts Study Centre, University for the Creative Arts at Farnham
The Textiles Collection, University College for the Creative Arts at Farnham
The Textiles Collection at The Whitworth Art Gallery, Manchester
IPC Media
James Weir
Jane Weir
as detailed in the Appendix

All rights reserved. This book is sold subject to the condition
that it shall not, by way of trade or otherwise, be lent, resold, hired out
or otherwise circulated without the publisher's prior consent, in any form
of binding or cover other than that in which it is published and without
a similar condition including this condition being imposed on
the subsequent purchaser.

For permission to reprint or broadcast these poems write to
Templar Poetry

A CIP catalogue record of this book is available
from the British Library.

Typeset by Pliny
Graphics by Paloma Violet
Printed and bound in Wales
by
Gomer Press, Llandysul, Ceredigion

Author's Note

This book is not a narrative biography and like much of Barron and Larcher's work is innovative and experimental. The poems, textiles and images which appear together tell their stories, they do not merely illustrate.

Acknowledgements

I wish to thank everyone who has helped in the course of researching and writing this book. Many thanks to Jean Vacher, Collections Manager at the Crafts Study Centre, Farnham, Surrey and Frances Pritchard, Curator of Textiles at the Whitworth Art Gallery in Manchester who enabled my research on Phyllis Barron and Dorothy Larcher's textiles to grow and flourish. I also wish to acknowledge the work that Robin and Heather Tanner carried out during their lives to collect a thoroughly documented archive of Phyllis Barron and Dorothy Larcher's work, and related material which has been invaluable in providing detail of their practical work and lives. I wish to thank Tanya Harrod, Barley Roscoe and Sheila Harvey for advice on specific details relating to cloth and photographs. Also the wonderful *Selvedge* for first publication of two of the poems and part of the Foreword of the book. I wish to thank my family and friends in England, Ireland and Italy for their continuing support, and especially Dorothy - 'keep talking textiles'. Finally I thank Phyllis Barron, Dorothy Larcher along with Enid Marx, Margaret Lambert and Ethel Mairet, whose work remains a source of sustenance and inspiration.

Foreword

'I think 'fabric' is the most disgusting word in the English language. When people tell me they're doing 'fabric printing' I feel I'd like to kick them.'

Phyllis Barron

My journey into handblock printing began several years ago, in Venice, when I was researching the pioneering work of Mariano Fortuny, his experiments in block printing, alongside natural dyeing techniques, particularly indigo. One evening a friend of mine gave me a copy of Fiona McCarthy's biography of the life and work of William Morris, knowing my interest in textiles, specifically in the Arts and Crafts movement. The more I read, the more I became astonished by Morris's manic industriousness, his insatiable appetite to 'discover' and 'make'; especially since part of this 'making' included writing up to a thousand lines of verse a day. Morris's letters show that the writing of poems had become obsessive. In his poetic phase the urge to make a poem came nagging at him constantly like one of his compulsive physical activities; a mental equivalent of netting and weaving.

He expressed lucid views on how other poets approached the making of their poetry: 'Shelley had no eyes' and Keats he found easy to relate to because of his 'supreme visual quality.' Of Keats's poem 'The Skylark' he said, 'WHAT a gorgeous thing it is!' Morris saw this poem as an entity 'made' up - like a textile - from its elements, the words, lines, rhythms, rhymes, cadences and so on threaded together by Keats's 'eye'. He also drew a distinction between 'poets of rhetoric... such as Milton and Swinburne and poets who were primarily makers of pictures, visually observant poets such as Chaucer and Keats.'

The poetry canon is littered with poets who, as with all great artists, practised the tradition of close and accurate observation, such as the detail of cytology in some of the work of American poet Marianne Moore; whose poetic engineering of scientific process and detail into the heart of her poetry gives the work its fine complexity and insights. The English poet, Gerald Manley Hopkins, with his sprung rhythm in verse, may be regarded as creating the poetic equivalent of a woven welsh blanket, with the formal and strict symmetries of fine close woven patterns. In short there are parallels and affinities in the making of a poem and the making of a textile, which Morris clearly recognised.

Although Morris's approach to 'making' later moved away from traditional methods and ideals towards producing his designs with industrial modes of manufacture, using newly emerging chemical dyes and machinery, many contemporary textile artists, particularly women, continued to create their work with traditional hand making methods. They used labour intensive production where the artist had close contact with the raw fibres, handspun threads, handmade textiles and the natural dyestuffs which served as the palette for their designs. Among these women were the weaver and dyer Ethel Mairet, the embroiderer Eve Simmonds and the block printers Phyllis Barron and Dorothy Larcher. They were pioneers of natural dyeing and were, with others, responsible for recovering and reintroducing natural dyes into fine art and design.

It was the language of the patterned textiles of Barron and Larcher that drew me to the making of the poems that inhabit this book; the unique rhythms, rhymes, repeats and the conversations running through their printed stuffs. Each length of cloth, which they named like a person or a particular place, sometimes the very spirit and essence of a place, appears to take on a personality, which in turn seems to posses a distinct voice, speaking in its own tone, expressing its own mood with its own inflections. Indeed many of their prints, I felt, looked far beyond the initial impulse of representation and startled, altering perception, like language or words stitched together can so often do.

At times it was as though the block and print were both the mouth and the menu for the feast. And what a complex feast it was, punctuated with conversations of all kinds, sometimes quiet, at others jostling; though never vying or breaking the harmonies between the nuance of the movement of the block and the finality of design, colour and texture. Even on some of the overprints I never sensed direct competition, just a working out of something through the print. And where one pattern is bold and abstract you are just as likely to find another that is quiet or contemplative, like a psalm or hymn flushed with subtle cadences. There are also fragilities and imperfections that resonate. So often the language of any art is not quite enough; it discomposes, yet does not completely express what it needs to, teasing at the unconscious before it soaks away. This effect is visible in the work of Barron and Larcher, particularly in their experimental pieces. Sometimes the narrative or story is told with starling clarity; at others the patterning fuzzes, fades away, making something not quite heard.

It is interesting seeing their patterns printed on different kinds of cloth, how the dialogues or monologues alter depending on the context; silk brocade, crepe de chine, linen, cotton, or velvet. And in different lights the emphasis often shifts, and very like a poem read in different rooms to different people, patterns the air in such a way that it is always received differently.

Sometimes you discover poems, something heard or seen or read breaking away like bread. Barron and Larcher did this too, exploring and experimenting with the idea of what a block is and what it could achieve. They used found objects, such as car mats, kitchen utensils, mollusc shells, cotton reels and seed heads, conjuring a kind of magic out of the ordinary and by so doing transformed the nature of shape and line and contour with colour. Experimentation and play characterised their approach to developing their designs, reflecting the philosophy of Robin Tanner, the teacher and etcher and a close friend, who believed in the connection between play, creativity and work. The design philosophy of Ethel Mairet - think in cloth, not on paper - was reflected in the way Barron and Larcher worked through their design and production processes. A significant range of their textiles have survived, including the 'Girton curtains', because they used durable stuffs to dye and print.

Barron and Larcher were part of the English revival of hand block printing that followed the second Post Impressionist Exhibition in 1912, organised by the artist and critic Roger Fry. There was a powerful resurgence of activity in the British Arts and Crafts movement, with an emphasis on traditional modes of production, which led directly to the formation of the Omega Workshop group of artists by Fry and the development of several other important communities of collaborative workers between the two wars and after, including Enid Marx, Paul Nash, the Footprints group, Crysede, Cresta, Susan Bosence and Yately Industries. Their printed textiles embraced the eclecticism of modernity through movements such as Vorticism, with an emphasis on movement through image and its abstraction on cloth.

Barron and Larcher's work, combining traditional production methods of hand block printing and vegetable dyeing with their avant-garde designs, attracted substantial commissions from a range of wealthy and influential clients. Although their strict adherence to traditional handmade production methods limited the volume of their output, it did not diminish the range or diversity of their designs. The significance of their work in contemporary art was recognised by critics like Roger Fry who commented in *Vogue* (1926) that 'something of the native grain survives in these stuffs.. some vital quality that has not been pressed and stamped and tortured.'

At a recent reading there were a couple of women knitting in the audience. It was wonderful. I read one of my poems 'Hand Knits' to them as a sort of offering. The faint dolphin clicks of the needles resonated with the sound of my own voice. What more could I ask - except for it to be repeated!

Bibliography

Anscombe, I., *A Woman's Touch, Women in Design from 1860 to the Present Day*, Virago, 1984.
Barron, Phyllis, *My Life as a Block Printer*, unpublished transcript taken by Heather Tanner of a talk given at Dartington, April 1964.
Barron, Phyllis, *The Block Printing Of Cover Paper*, Dryad Handicrafts, Leicester, 1928.
Bosence, S., *Hand Block Printing & Resist Dyeing*, David & Charles, 1985
Coatts, M., *A Weaver's Life, Ethel Mairet 1872 - 1952*, Crafts Study Centre, Bath, 1983.
Fry, R., in *Vogue*, 1926
Greensted, M., *Arts and Crafts Movement in the Cotswolds*, Sutton Publishing, 1993.
Harrod, T., *The Crafts in Britain in the 20th Century*, Yale University Press, 1999
Jackson, L., *20th Century Pattern Design: Textile & Wallpaper Pioneers*, Mitchell Beazley, 2002.
McCarthy, F., *William Morris, A Life for Our Time*, Faber & Faber, 1994.
Powers, A., *Modern Block Printed Textiles*, Walker Books, 1992.
Roscoe, B., *The Biggest And Simplest Results*, essay on the commission of Girton College, Cambridge, in Crafts No 144, Jan - Feb, 1997.
Seaby, W. A., *Colour Printing With Linoleum And Wood Blocks*, Dryad Handicrafts, Leicester, 1928.
Tanner, R., *What I Believe: Lectures and other Writing*, Crafts Study Centre, 1989.
Weir, J., *Cytology and the Strawberry Plant in the Poetry of Marianne Moore*, Unpublished essay, 2004.

Other Reading

Evans, M., *Missing Persons: The impossibility of auto/biography*, Routledge, 1999.
Faderman, L., *Surpassing the Love of Men: Romantic Frienships and Love Between Women from the Renaissance to the Present,* Womens' Press, 1981.
Holmes, R., Shelley: *The Pursuit,* Weidenfeld & Nicolson, 1974.
Holmes, R., *Footsteps: Adventures of a Romantic Biographer*, Hodder & Stoughton, 1985.
Polkey, P. (Ed.) *Womens' Lives Into Print: The Theory, Practice and Writing of Feminist Auto/Biography*, Macmillan Press Ltd, 1999.
Spender, D., *Women Of Ideas (And what men have done to them)* Routledge & Kegan Paul, 1982.
Stanley, L., *The Auto/biographical I: The theory and practice of Auto/biography*, Manchester University Press, Manchester, 1992.
Tóibín, C., *Love in a Dark Time: Gay Lives From Wilde To Almodóvar,* Picador, 2001.
Tóibín, C., *Lady Gregory's Toothbrush,* Picador, 1988.
Tóibín, C., *The Master,* Picador, 2004.
Woolf, V., *Flush*, Hogarth Press, 1933.
Woolf, V., *Women and Writing,* Womens' Press Ltd, 1979

Historically, psychologically, intellectually... I should like to know how many women there are who have honestly no story to tell, how many have some other story than the one which alone is supposed to count and how many of those who think it worth their while to dissect themselves are in a position to tell all they know of the result.

Edith Simcox, Autobiography of a Shirt Maker, 17 October 1887.

We walk about, well wadded with stupidity. We have to. If we had but keen vision and feeling... it would be like hearing the grass grow and the squirrel's heartbeat, and we should die of that roar which lies on the other side of silence.

George Eliot

Contents

Poetry

Montreuil - sur - Mer, Normandy Blocks	1
French Peasant Woman	4
Encountering Toile On The Way To The Slade	7
Dye Books	10
Indigo Cloth With White Stutters	12
Mollusc Shells	14
Smock Puzzle	16
White Spots And Splashes	18
Flock	20
Experiments With An Old French Block Using Nitric Acid To Discharge Colour On Lengths Of Indigo Dyed Cotton	22
Natural Dye Colours	24
Preparation In The Kitchen, Attempt At An Indigo Vat	27
A Dyer's Thoughts On Looking At Plain Cottons, Linens And Hessians Wedged Between Imported Goods	30
Most Of My Experiments, My Early Prints	32
When The Indigo Flowers	34
Haul	36
Air On Indigo	38

A Part Of Me Recognises This Too, Morris Thinking About Brown Instead Of Indigo Blue	40
Log	42
1916, Working With Alizarin In A Field Hospital Belgium	44
Painting Luminous Compass Dials For The Royal Flying Corps	46
At Gospels Ethel Looks At Samples Sent	48
Clifford	50
Advice On Cutting A Block	53
A Tiger Against The Mouth Of Ajanta Caves, 1914	56
Accompanying Lady Herringham At The Ajanta Caves	58
Lizard	60
Evening Dew And Morning Air	62
When Dorothy Met Phyllis, Brook Street Gallery	64
Carnac	67
Basket	70
Overprint Thrush Over Todd	72
Nasturtiums	74
Entranced	76
Portrait Of An Evacuee Dress	79
Printed Stuffs And Suggia's Dress	82

Girton Curtains	85
Cushions For Coco Chanel	88
Coco Asks, Could You Print Ankle Bracelets On Woollen Stockings?	91
The Duke Of Westminster's Boar	94
For Flying Cloud We Thought Large Or Old Captain	96
Marx	99
Painswick Dandelions	103
Mahogany Boat Seats With Infinite Possibilities	106
In The French Alps, Phyllis Eats A Marmot	108
Phyllis Barron's Hat	110
Dyes Racing	112
Pastry Cutter	114
There Was A Cloth, Sadly Now Lost, And We Called It Scaffold	116
Gathering Home Grown Flowers From Our Painswick Garden	118
There, In An Ercol Bottom Drawer	121

Contents

Textiles & Images
(All appear on pages facing)

Natural Unbleached Linen	1
French Unbleached Cotton, Hand Block Print	2
"French Spot", Indigo Discharge on Heavy Natural Linen	4
"French Toile", with narrative	7,8
Dye Books	10
Unnamed, Unused Cotton	12
"Scallop", Length of Galled Linen with positive block print in iron	14
"Mairet", Indigo Discharge on Cotton	16
"Lyon", Indigo discharge on Heavy Natural Linen	18
"Railway", Positive Print in Iron on Linen, with red V- design added	20
"Winchester", Printed on Heavy Natural Linen	22
"Small Feather", Indigo discharge on Natural Linen	24
The Indigo Vat	27
Diagram - Indigo Steamers	28
Hessian	30
"Diamond", Positive Block Print in Black and Brown on Natural Cotton	32
"Girton", Indigo Discharge on Linen	34
"Hazlitt", Indigo Discharge on White Cotton	36
"Christmas", On Fine Natural Linen	38

"Elizabethan", Length of White Balloon Cotton with Indigo Discharge Print — 40

"Log", Iron on Linen — 42

'Pip' & 'Spot', Positive Print in Red Chemical Dye on Unbleached Linen — 44

Compass: mounted on the upper wing of the Bristol F2B Fighter — 46

"Dent", Printed in Red on Heavy Undyed Linen — 48

"Clifford", Real Alizarin on Fine Natural Silk — 50

Printing Blocks Used by
Phyllis Barron and Dorothy Larcher, Circa 1927 — 53

Gouges and Knife — 54

"Delhi", Printed in iron and synthetic red on buff Handwoven Cotton:
This is thought to be the only remaining fragment of this piece — 56

Paisley Shawl, Handblock Printed on Silk — 58

"Lizard", Indigo Discharge on Handwoven Cotton — 60

Phyllis Barron & Dorothy Larcher, shopping in a French Market (1930's) — 62

"Chestnut", Printed in Brown on Natural Linen — 64

"Carnac", Indigo Discharge on White Cotton — 67, 68

"Basket", Unbleached Linen with a positive print in Black — 70

"Thrush Over Todd", Positive Block Print, "Todd"
on natural linen, overprinted with "Thrush" — 72

Detail from Copper Jardiniere — 74

"Butterfly", Iron on Undyed Balloon Cotton — 76

Dress, In "Little Flower" — 79

"Little Flower", Rust on Ballon Cotton — 80

"French Dot", Probably on Natural Holland Steeped in Powdered
Oak Galls, Printed With Old French Blocks With Copper Pins   82

"Small Feather", Printed in Black, Red Spot Design Added   85, 86

"Chanel", Fragment   88

"Spine", Printed in Blue on Undyed Organdie   91, 92

"Wild Boar", Detail From a Line Drawing   94

"Flying Cloud", The Duchess's sitting room, all loose covers and
curtains designed and printed by Phyllis Barron   96

Banksia Fruit   99

Unnamed block printed in rust on buff velvet, overprinted
in black with "Fishbone" and a pastry cutter   100

Walking the Block at Painswick   103

"Octopus", Composed of three blocks, printed in Grey, Red and Black   104

"Large Captain", Printed in Cutch on Natural Linen   106

Muff (1920's) with Handblock Printed Silk Lining   108

Phyllis Barron and Dorothy Larcher, shopping in a French Market   110

Pastry Wheel Print   112

Pastry Cutters   114

"Derbyshire Scaffold"   116

Long Basket   118

"Jasmine"
Printed in Black over an unnamed block printed in yellow in White Cotton
Printed in black on crepe silk over bands of red dots
Printed in red on Balloon Cloth
Printed in blue on Fine Silk   121, 124

Montreuil - sur - Mer, Normandy Blocks

'I was mad to know how they really worked'
                                        Phyllis Barron

In your arms you carry
what looks like hewn blocks of Irish peat -
though it's August and we've no need of a fire.
Sun blasted after a stint of sketching
I watch as you dump block after block.
A closer look tells me they're too deformed
to be peat and have the soft spongy thud
of fruit wood; perhaps cherry or lime.

They're too eccentric - in part,
too ornate, for a child's building blocks,
and they lack colour, except inside wells
and ridges, where traces of pigment
hide as hair dye does behind ear lobes;
only curiously they're not ear lobes,
more like merging hives or welts
that at first sight make no sense.

I have to stop myself, check,
because this incessant turning,
this passing through the hands,
flipping each block from side to side
to see what's missing
is silly and I should be sketching.

Yet there are makeshift handles,
tiny pins strategically placed.
A penny drops. A twig snaps.
Neats of half buds present
a berry, a floret, a leaf.
Of course, they're blocks for cloth - not paper.

Sculpting a ripe pear after dinner
I find myself thinking -
as the evening sun
mopped black by the sky
dries moonlight across the table -
that perhaps I can make them speak.

Neats were popular small-scale floral or geometric motifs and a staple in the textile industry in France during the second half of the nineteenth century.

French Peasant Woman

The wick ignites. A flame
whimpers apricot, wakes me.
A peasant woman stands
at the bottom of my bed.
I can't be sure what region
she comes from, though
it's probably the upper Auvergne,
her gown looks homespun,
her bodice covered by foulard
looks gritty and invincible.

Around her head a carousel reels:
geese, hens, black pom-pom banties,
ducklings dusted with pollen.
Her arms are full,
full of monogrammed linens,
full of metisse and chanvre,
rough cut, bursting to the pail
with what looks like rendered
cattle jaws of print blocks,
and her arms extended
are brimming, are endless,
like a lover when he first enters.

Her speckled kisses leave me climbing
with bulging runner beans,
flushes of scarlet flowers
which I'll store in some abstract way,
before travelling the broad length,
back to London.

Metisse is a mix of cotton and linen, chanvre is coarse hemp.

Encountering Toile On The Way To The Slade

'I was at the Slade, where you were only encouraged to draw the human form with a hard pencil, and if I made any suggestions of anything like textile printing I think I should have been turned out at once.'
Phyllis Barron

I've walked this street
so many times
that the distance
that once mystified
has become mundane,
has simplified.

But today as I drive the pace,
keep time with the swing
of my pear-drop earrings,
today the streetscape
becomes an allegory.

As far as the eye can see
figures stroll, feet strapped
with pattens.
A bolt of Toiles de Jouy,
in palest duck egg blue,
along the selvedge,
a river laced by birches
that like a stomacher
bows and elongates.

A place were legions
of valerian, squads
of dandelions,
devise tormented botanies,
so stylised
birds might preen.

Overhead the sky hangs,
a heavy balloon
popped by a steeple;
ochre rain smokes.

I retreat
inside a doorway
until the rain appeases.
But the scene reins tighter,
until - like a chair fitted
with a loose cover -
I'm scarcely breathing.

Toile de Jouy is used mainly for furnishings, covers and draperies; toile meaning simple or linen cloth. Since the mid-eighteenth century the term also refers to large scale engraved scenic designs that decorate fabrics. Designs may be political, historical, literary, as well as representing everyday life. They are most often copper plated or roller printed and predominately use the colours, red, blue, black, puce and sepia.

Dye Books

'So I went to the British Museum, but it wasn't the place for me –
I was very soon shot out of there and went to the Victoria and Albert Museum.'
                                                                    Phyllis Barron

Experimental Researches concerning the Philosophy of Permanent colours
and the best means of producing them by dyeing, calico printing etc.
                                                        Edward Bancroft, 1794

A practical hand book of dyeing and calico printing
                                                        William Crooks, 1874

The Principle and Practice of Textile Printing and Dyeing
                                        Edmund Knecht and James Fothergill, 1912

A trip to the Patent Office, for descriptions in full,
into the nature of dye ingredients and its processes.

Without this a dye cannot be patented.

Afterwards sipping Saxon Blue in a teashop
thinking about plants that dye purple, such as bryony,
damson, blaeberry, sundew, deadly nightshade

whilst the rain outside inks.

Saxon blue is a dye made by indigo dissolved in oil of vitriol

Indigo Cloth With White Stutters

'..if you read a thing five times you began to know a little bit what it meant, and then if you started to do some experiments you found out a good deal more.'

Phyllis Barron

Tomorrow I'll try
the Patents Office,
in the hope they'll shed
some light,
because I've no idea
how dyeing is done.

I shrink beneath
the turtle shell of my eider,
visualise an indigo cloth,
discharged,
birth marked,
white and white and white.

In no time I'm back on the market,
watching the way
the primitive dress prints
of peasant women
scoff at the rich,
doffing fancy manufactured.

This affinity of blueness
the cloth has with cornflowers
leaves me pondering how I might
capture not only its blueness,
but the hundred or so stutters
of white that pucker like trout kisses,
the infinite prairie of its surface.

Mollusc Shells

We think we know so much…

yet the dog scavenging
shellfish on the beach
barked in a language
we couldn't decipher,

and we were puzzled
by its purple muzzle,
stiff peaks of violet foaming
between nooks and crevices
of its canines.

Small sacs removed from mollusc shells contain a white glutinous liquid which yields Tyrian purple.

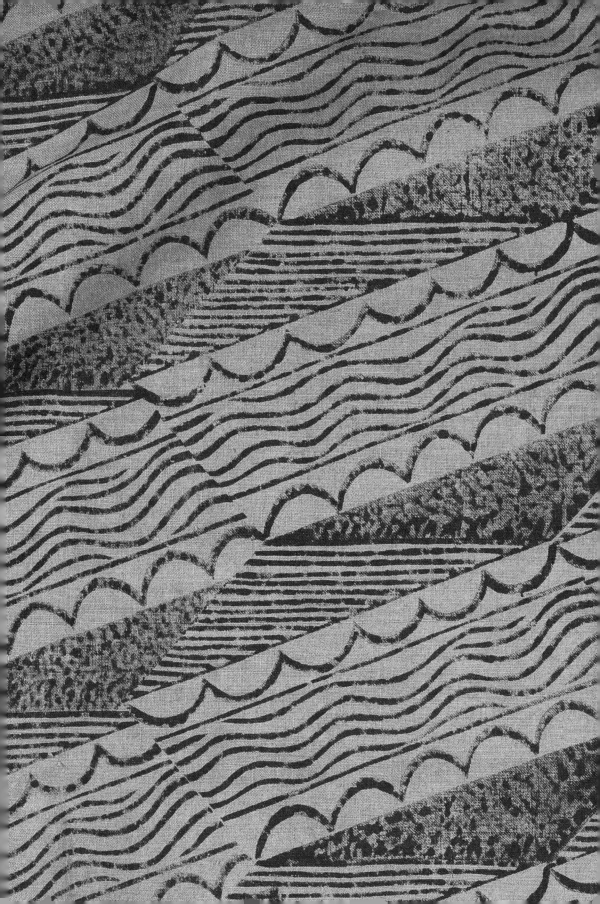

Smock Puzzle

The light ploughs across
Thérèse's workbench
left strewn with etchings.
From the back of a door
her pocked blue smock hangs,
a sting ray,
gamekeeper's warning.
White spots and splashes
of nitric acid bloom like fungi,
and I wonder if they're
symptomatic of the deep water
blue that makes up the cloth
of the smock's surface,
or if it has nothing
whatsoever to do with colour.
For instance, if the smock were red
or yellow would the population
of spots and splashes stabilise or spread?

Thérèse Lessore was an accomplished etcher and painter, who was married to the painter Bernard Adeney, a friend of Phyllis Barron. Thérèse later became the wife of the painter Walter Sickert.

White Spots And Splashes

When Thérèse returned she explained
that her smock was made from cotton
dyed from the plant *Indigofera*.
Hoisting it over her head,
she spread her hand across the cloth,
like the flat blade of a palate knife
as if smoothing batter for a crepe.

I'll never forget
the tilt of the studio window,
the sight of Thérèse ogling light
like a scented geranium cutting,
matter of fact,
saying - *look how the spots and splashes*
mesmerise like a song thrush's breast,
explaining - *they're the rainfall*
of nitric acid when etching,
and it's this that causes the dye
to discharge white against blue ground -
at any rate, that's the basic effect.

Thérèse bought her indigo smocks from The Friends of Armenia, a sort of missionary society who imported the stuff. Phyllis Barron initially bought some of her cotton from there.

Flock

I stand in front of the print table.
There's the sound of pitch pine breathing
beneath a length of blanched stuff,
long face of a Puritan stiffening,
that I'll soon print into oblivion.

I can hardly hold the cut block in my hand,
all the weight, pressure of a demanding run.
This exercise, I tell myself, is hard learned.
Should I have accepted the good advice
and flocked, covered the face of the block
with layers of fine fibres, before printing or not?

I remember the landing, dull thud
as a block was mallet-struck.
The way the print sat, too firm, too even.
I wrestled for a long time
before leaping toward the grain,
the hard grating sound,
of dye paste in direct contact,
of limitless starvation and dried out-ness.

Traditionally block printers would cover the face of a block with a fine layer of wool known as flocking before charging the block with dye paste. This technique produced a fine and even print. However Phyllis Barron experimented with dye paste directly applied to the block and did not flock because she preferred the sparse finish on cloth printed without the mediation of flock.

**Experiments With An Old French Print Block
Using Nitric Acid To Discharge Colour
On Lengths Of Indigo Dyed Cotton**

When the indigo lengths finally settle,
and the block with its simple geometric design
starts to remember, what cuts and gouges
mean to the sweep of the hand,
the shadow that follows the bent head;
then and only then do I attempt a final print.
Across the table, all those endless days,
endless nights of messy rehearsal -
first with the Russians, then the French,
all those endless days and nights
of working and re-working, of musing,
of wrestling, of finally taking from the wall
one of the best I'd ever seen. I can hardly look
at that exquisite French block, and yes,
to think that even then I nearly ruined its sparse face,
that seasons ago launched a dress craze.
To think I nearly spoiled everything,
and all because I didn't yet understand
the difference between liquid and paste,
and what that meant; at least the effect
on cotton printing. But now I see,
see that nitric acid needs, like different
kinds of love, to be diluted,
if it's to make any kind of sense.

Natural Dye Colours

'Bancroft thrilled me very much'

Phyllis Barron

After reading and re-reading
Bancroft's descriptions -
he reads like Tolstoy -
for the use and application
of iron rust, I took my chance,
experimented with recipes
for iron black, powdered oak galls,
cutch brown. Haven't you guessed?
Delved even deeper into indigo.

I signed up to natural linen cloth,
short lengths and colour combinations
which gave me courage and strength -
like a frontier family - to carry on.
And the result? I turned a corner
into infinity, and it was like something
you'd dreamed, seeing
wild flowers in a field far outstrip rapeseed.

Preparation In The Kitchen, Attempt At An Indigo Vat

'working with indigo was the biggest thrill of my life'

Phyllis Barron

I improvised,
gathered together utility pieces,
that might for the mean time do.

Equipment such as:
chipped enamel bowls, dust rags,
wooden utensils, pans, an old gas ring,
a dustbin, pegs and jugs,
a strong clothes line for drip drying, a hose,
long rubber gloves, a Belfast sink.

I found a place for the dyestuff;
an importer down by the docks,
who - to his credit - knew his stuff.

Embedded in my head other recipes
I'd learnt to recite with the might of psalms:
iron black, powered oak galls,
cutch brown and indigo,
having seen with my own eyes
the transformation on cottons and linens.

I filled the dustbin with warm water,
sprinkled a dessert spoon
of hydrosulphite, stirred.

In a pudding basin I prepared stock solution.
In the following order: three cups of sea salt,
one cup of caustic soda, dissolved whilst stirring in
one cup of water, one and a half cups of indigo grains,
two more cups of water.

Waited.

Waited, for the dark blue iridescent scum,
its clear yellow liquid coiling below.
Avoid air in vat. Pour without splashing.

Stir.

In another pail I housed a solution
for wetting, composed of some sort
of neutral detergent such as teepol,
to one gallon of warm water.

Wetted.

For overalls I bought lengths
of hand woven raw cloth
from an Armenian shop in Hampstead,
consulted what I thought
the best out-of-print books.

Now all to do was spread the word
amongst my friends, put in the post a bottle
and a note saying -
I need night urine, in buckets provided please!
Ignite the flame, stand over - don't stop stirring.

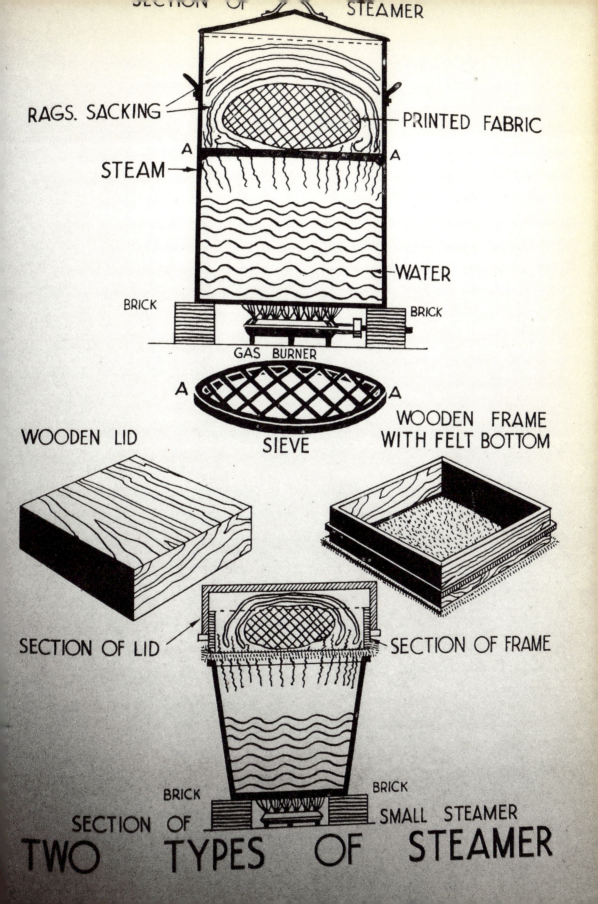

A Dyer's Thoughts On Looking At Plain Cottons, Linens And Hessians Wedged In Between Imported Goods

Down by the docks, waiting in the goods yard
for dyestuff, I'm aware of the presence
of tangerines, palm stencilled dates, crates of Indian tea,
African coffee, mass-market blue and white plates,
stacked like Whitstable oysters, the air singed by spices.
I'm also aware, and these days increasingly so,
by what lies sandwiched between.
Rough cuts of natural hemp and linen sacking
that knowingly - like antiquity Gods - know
instinctively the ways of these goods.
Crumpled squares that soothe the rough,
leave well alone, keep well apart for great distances.
Am I insane lingering on the humble cloth or does pure
thought grasp at the chance of a natural affinity?

Most Of My Experiments, My Early Prints

were with cutch on unbleached calico.
I strived, kept the materials clean and simple,
humble like bread and cheese,
practical; sleeve rather than a handkerchief.
I scavenged bits of wartime balloon cotton,
grey linen prison sheets purchased from Mrs Lubin
in the Caledonian market,
and spread out my repertoire
inside an improvisation
of a photographer's printing tray.

When The Indigo Flowers

High summer.
I stare into the indigo vat,
sloshing,
a cabochon of deep
delphinium blue,
in mint condition
like a brand new dress
before the tag's torn off.

Nothing can prepare you
for the accumulation
of snorting bronze bubbles
that pitter-patter
across its dense centre,
or the tiniest light blue bubbles
that complete
the shape of two tiaras crowning;
nothing can compete.

I serve the flower - holy with two hands.
In awe I skim the flower
before baptising blue, a length of wetted cloth.

Haul

If you can, work outside
where there's a breeze - do.

Let sunlight clip
in the old-fashioned way
at your ears, as though you're
a Hardy field walker child.

What better way to see
a length of silk or cotton
dredged from the depths
of an indigo vat?

Watch as it's rinsed,
squeezed
before being unfolded,

held out by a skilled woman,
a fruit bat wing.

Air On Indigo

Fine-tune the clothesline,
then using your finger -
pluck
the string of a cello.

Begin to peg.
Take care,
as like a tendon
it may snap.

Distract.
Grab a stool,
a bowl of bloated peas
in need of shelling.

Give the hands -
as well as the head
something fitting to do,

while you watch
the cotton billow,
come greenish blue,
allow 60 seconds -
blue,
come blue, bluer

Blue.

A Part Of Me Recognises This Too,
Morris Thinking About Brown Instead Of Indigo Blue

*'I used not to mind being blue myself, and when I wore my own indigo
my underclothes were always blue, but when my customers complained
I told them it was only surface dye and would wear off.'*

Phyllis Barron

To take his mind off blue
it was said that Morris went fishing
in the river at Kelmscott,
and for a short while his thoughts
were lost to the swirl and refractions.

Though he wore a coat of old moleskin -
plant equations for brown
seeped inside his head,
such as walnut husks with root green nuts,
layers of onion skins,
the barks of alder, birch, oak,
handfuls of larch pine needles,
hop stalks, red currants with alum,
baskets of water lily roots,
the whortleberry's tender shoots ,
and nut galls, scrunch of dulse,
frazzled lichens.

His legs sank into the bank,
he held his fishing rod
against the willow bough,
his hands and upper arms
so dunked in indigo they made a show.
Come late afternoon, a kingfisher
alighted on his wrist, a gift of glints -
only the trained eye could distinguish.

Log

Midwinter: all around
trees stand, branches plead.
In my brogues, man's overcoat, arms akimbo
I watch men load stumps of silver birch,
beech logs into a Jekyll wheelbarrow,
marvelling that moonlight
armour plates trees in such a way.

The men are nearly done.
I stoop, retrieve a stray beech log,
feel the gravitas course beneath its grain;
the perfect size, fit for a novice hand.
Saved from the hearth's blaze
I feel I owe a debt with each cut,
each gouge made
to the harmonies of the seed
out of which this print block
is first named.

1916, Working With Red In A Field Hospital, Belgium

Back in the workshop I look
for any kind of flux, discrepancy,
or break from the uniform,
when dyeing wild madder with gromwell,
or common sorrel with bedstraw - but not here.

The men lie, abstract shapes and sizes
angled and shattered in beds,
a fraction between types and ages.
Without exception all dye red,
grimy sheets, make-do blankets.

I notice little variation in shade
or depth of shade, or length of spread or seep,
or smear or splatter,
or where the bandage unravels,
or the flesh stitches bloom and split.

Take this boy - he won't mind me showing you -
His wound replicates early nineteenth century anilines -
look closely at his right buttock,
see mauve going green, going flinch black.
No amount of handiwork can stop
the corruption that imprints flesh;
there are no mordants for miles around.

**Painting Luminous Compass Dials
For The Royal Flying Corps**

I work in the dark
paint on photographs,
degrees, letters on dials.
I do what's asked methodically.
Mr Hughes says,
Men mustn't scrunch
up their eyes to read.

The radium salt and varnish
are difficult to mix and slip,
though after countless experiments
I soon get the knack -
suddenly
the steady rings of glow-worms.

Occasionally, my hand shakes,
leaves me wondering, will I ever conquer
the tremors that Singer-sew
through my fingertips.

Some days I sense it crouched inside
the tuned instruments of my wrists.
So I fix my thoughts on textile samples
sent to *Gospels,*
hoping the dyer Ethel

will know - will understand -
that from her book,
Vegetable Dyes,
come thoughts of paradise
fit for a Keat's skylark.

At Gospels Ethel Looks At Samples Sent

This morning looking
at samples you sent
an oil lamp glowed within.
Between my fingers
rubbing each square
like French lavender
I'm thinking *why*
must there be an end?
I lay each sample on an oak desk
as if they were pieces
of fine cut marquetry,
or slithers of peel
cut for January marmalade.

All have distinct features,
some show discrete
and subtle references,
though these, thank God,
are in the minority.
And I can see, although
I don't agree, how for some,
blatant originality scares.
I inch closer, hold up
a sample called *Log*,
invite my eye to twin
with natural light and stare.

An hour or so passes.
With my shuttle
I'm weaving you a note
in pure linen,
demonstrating vigour and strength -
Yes, if it's at all possible, do send some lengths,
they're simply, simply wonderful.

Ethel Mairet (1872 - 1952), a highly regarded weaver and dyer exhibited with Phyllis Barron several times at the Brook Street Gallery, London. She experimented with handspun yarns and unusual materials doing much to revive the tradition of vegetable dyeing.

Clifford

Hands motor scissors through my hair,
nimble fingers spread, angle, trap and snip.
I stare at my feet as strands fall free.

A door opens.

At first I see a nursery narrative of sorts,
a series of geometric gingerbread men,
all starfishing across a painted floor.

A door closes, a door opens.

Gusts separate and rearrange each strand.
I think alizarin, white as emphasis.
I shake my head and turn.
From the broad window
lashings of nitric acid rain
serrate the busy pavement edge,
and all that does not leap and bound seems dead.

Alizarin - the red dye derived from the root of the madder plant.

Advice On Cutting A Block

*'success depends not on learning to do what is difficult,
but in finding out what is easy.'*
Phyllis Barron

There are many things I could say
about materials you could use.
I have seen miraculous prints come
from potatoes, windfalls of orchard apples,
from a cake slicer a pattern that looked
like shoals of lemon sole.
I've been privy to prints
from sea shells, ribs of a dolly tub.
I have printed with rubber mats
from a motorcar, from a pastry cutter.

Let's see, for the beginner
battleship Linoleum is good,
not as hard on the hands as wood.
In time you get a feeling
for the material,
and come to know
that a fine print requires pear wood,
that the fate of the overall pattern
is literally - in your hands;
the shape of the block is crucial.

Rectangles should be avoided.

Yes, rectangles should be avoided,
because a straight line cuts
like an easterly wind
right through the design,
and the eye sees only squares advancing.

Again, this is for the beginner,
and as a rule - I'd say best simplify.

Keep the drawing flat,
cut as soon as possible.
Using a small block as a shape,
coax, develop your design.
In time, it becomes instinctive,
knowing what will
or will not work,
knowing how abstracts skip,
repeat, like a lioness's heartbeat.

With linoleum, take a fine,
sharp-pointed knife,
outline the whole
of your drawing deeply.
Cut away with a gouge.

The background part
is left uncoloured.
Stick the cut design
with spirit shellac
onto a block of wood,
press with weights.

Fix the face.

Someday you'll get a shout
that roughly fits the hand,
that's easy to toy, manipulate -
Volta's inside your head.

Take it or leave it.

Fig. 1

Fig. 2

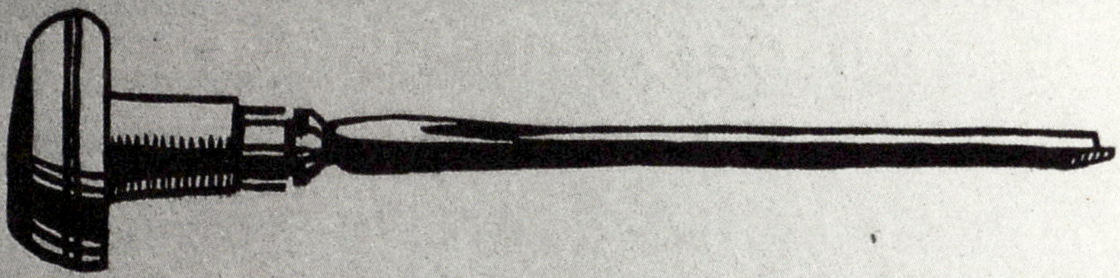

GOUGES

Fig. 3

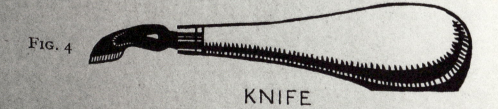

VARIOUS GOUGE SHAPES

Fig. 4

KNIFE

GOUGES AND KNIFE

Tiger Against The Mouth Of Ajanta Caves, 1914

Deep in the forest, orchids are virulent
and trees hard pressed between shafts
of porous sulphur light fight for posterity.

Ahead a guide rattlesnakes,
We soon be out, and we have to believe,
the heat's had us down a while and is killing.

Beneath our boots the foot of the gorge.
Below the Waghora river slakes a filthy petticoat.
Then we see, *There, there, to the right.*

Where?

There, there, to the right. On the far side of a loop,
tacked against the cliff, a tiger,
jade harlequins between stripes of black and ginger skin,

scabbed over like badly infected bayonet wounds.
And we send someone in front,
this time not armed with a gun,

but simply the skill to unpick,
without breeching the façade.

Dorothy Larcher accompanied Lady Herringham to India in 1914 to record Buddhist frescoes in the Ajanta Caves. Dorothy was unable to obtain transport home to England during the First World War, and remained in Calcutta, with an Indian family, teaching English. It was during this time that she learned about indigenous Indian dyeing and printing techniques.

Accompanying Lady Herringham At The Ajanta Caves

Inside the caves she contemplates the frescoes, *Miracle of Sarati,*
whilst I take notes, listen to her voice tap out verbatim;
and it's incredible, I know, yet this contrast between us works.
And although she has rigour, purpose, and I the verve to carry on
in heat, it seems to me, that she can't get beyond the vitality of surface -
of the chaityas and viharas of legends and divinities,
of the staccato sound of indigenous words spoken.

Now she is telling me, she would like to come at night,
enter its mouth when the last skid of orange disappears
and the fast flowing river burns at its edges like the ear
of someone being talked about, and she's telling me how,
armed with a net, a candle lit and lifted, she might see if streaked
gold goes red, is affected by the dizzying flight path of bats.

She is surface, all surface, cannot see what lies beyond
the fragmentary - that erosion is technique;
such as how the chisel struck, first the features of the rock,
made rough enough to hold the plaster, and as with the coming
of the rains, how plaster came into being,
made from clay, by a skilled hand, and how the finite drawing's
done in a flash, with colours applied - plaster wet,
so that in time, each colour succumbs to the figures
like desire, won't peel or decay, fades, fades, fades ever so.

Lizard

'I should love to meet the person who did it.'
Dorothy Larcher to Eve Simmonds

Coming into the room with Eve,
ever so quick, at first I didn't alight
upon the vigour of bite after bite,
of twisted white that basked over a rock of indigo.

How could I with embroideries
ringed, strewn around?
Some lay face down,
others flip-sided
on a sagging chair, arm of a sofa;
and I had to stop myself thinking -
as most embroiderers do -
that I prefer the wizardry
of the back to the front.

And it wasn't long before we settled,
as evening light
did amongst a play of bearded irises.
A moment kidnapped. An Indian dusk,
that in this country I'd not thought possible.
A garden in heat, strapped with Canna lilies
growing six feet in six seconds rather than a season.

A breeze off a yellowing broom brushes me back,
and I can see the crook of the old one printing,
Indian shot rattling around a wrist
as she strikes and releases, strikes and releases,
searing white hot, white hot, scattering lizards
from beneath a rock, as purple shadows
creep along the selvedge.

Indian shot are the seeds of the Canna lily, when dried they are used as beads for jewellery.
Eve Simmonds was an embroiderer and friend of Dorothy Larcher. This was the first time that Dorothy Larcher encountered the work of Phyllis Barron. The indigo discharge print was called 'Lizard' and was printed from an old French block.

Evening Dew And Morning Air

Inside the gallery the air
is thinly sliced as Parma ham.

Waiting for you,
what is there to do?

I step back
into my old India.

Searing days
spent on the banks
of a ginger river,

the women of Dacca
draping muslins
gifted Evening Dew and Morning air,

how no one dared to look for long
because they were so diaphanous.

When Dorothy Met Phyllis, Brook Street Gallery

'so Eve found me for her...'
                              Phyllis Barron

I stand inside the gallery, waiting.
Behind me hangs one of Ethel's weaves.
A knee rug, hand spun, a combination
of undyed and veg dyed,
which by the look - I'm only guessing -
I'd have to get up close, is a plain weave
crammed with weft stripes, blanket
stitched, furrows ploughed
until they're miles and miles away.

And there are several other woven pieces,
yet enough space left to complement
a good show case of hand blocked cloth,
and I recognise *Lizard* and *Log,*
dazzling, simply dazzling
in an understated way, while others
are new to me; although I can identify
her style anywhere; just as blindfold
you'd know hail hitting skin.

A door opens, the head of a tall oak sways
amongst a crowd of raw silk blouses blowing in,
and she is just as described,
her fingers long deckchair stripes,
slotting easily into the grooves of mine.

I'm wondering could we work together?
And you know the way a red sky spells snow -
I'm wondering could we work together?
Come clean.

Carnac

Dislocation, at first.

Wind ushers us randomly
toward long alignments,
scoured vertebrae of stones
hewn from local granite.

I watch you take off your glove
and with a finger trace the pox,
crusted with lichen - slow thinking.
And I can see little mouthfuls in your eyes.

I'm not touching, just tapping out
the pattern of a telegram inside my head.
Atlantic waves butter-curl
towards indented shoreline.

Shall I send it?

Back at base, over chocolate and mallows,
we meet in the middle.

We know that looks passed
between us in the workshop,
are sparks inside a diamond,
we know we have to get it right;
it's not enough visualising in daylight.
No.
We have to hold a vigil,
way past midnight,
until we harmonise.

In the yard we hose down
lengths of cotton indigo spat with stars.
We've left enough space to walk,
so we walk for miles,
even when we'd fixed on a short run.

The avenues are scraped back,
like tortoise shell combs
pulled through hair - and that's good.
Out there in the sun and the rain
each stone's a mimic.

Carnac is an ancient place in Southern Brittany. The area has a large assemblage of standing stones and other megalithic monuments. Phyllis Barron and Dorothy Larcher went to Carnac and the print is thought to have originated from avenues of stones and dolmens.

Basket

Printed in iron on ungalled linen,
this was the third block
I designed and cut,
and still as popular.

Today went something like this:
I pulled the light switch,
walked into the workshop ready to work.

On the bench a roll of stuff's been left out.
Ahead there's Carmen Miranda's basket
balancing - though without her head -
plain wicker stuffed
full of exotic fruit and flowers.

It's a bit like rotating pictures
around the house, you always think
why I never saw it like that before.

Is that a terrapin dancing
in time with a hummingbird
to the sweet music of longevity?

'Basket' was a print designed, cut and printed by Dorothy Larcher. It was one of her most popular prints.

Overprint Thrush Over Todd

We block printed Todd in iron black,
on a length of ungalled linen - stood back.
Abstracts sank upon the cloth,
as though they were soles of shoes
detached from feet.

There was something,
something about the shade, the hue,
rising like river mist, stringing us along like dew.
For sure it was nearly timeless
as a trench coat,
not as yet kit complete.

So mute, we gave the cloth to night.
Come dawn, despite poor daylight
spilling clove and cinnamon, despite -

we overprinted Thrush on Todd,
and for our time and patience
were rewarded with a quirky song
flush with repeats.

Nasturtiums

We talk about nasturtiums,
types of sprawling, climbing
and dwarf, such as *Tom Thumb*,
Whirlybird, *Alaska*, *Empress of India*,
Golden Jewel, *Ladybird*, *Mahogany Gleam*.

We talk deep, as if walking through drifts.
You shake out the memory of your mother.
How she gathered together
one whole colour, so they'd stand out,
being one block, inside a plain china vase.

You describe sugaring the flowers,
pickling green seeds to make poor man's capers.
I tell you how I do something similar with the leaf.

How I like to fly, maybe one or two
inside a copper spill, though sometimes
I do the same, same as your mother,
usually with hundreds of *Salmon Babies*.

Come spring I plant out packets
in copper pots wondering how they'll look,
crawling round the rim come summer,
clapping like cymbals come winter.

Don't be fooled or put off.
This is not a competition,
nobody wins or gets one over;
it's what some women still do.

Entranced

Often in arresting settings,
I'd happen upon you
meticulously turning a glass,
as if the glass were a globe,
then I know I have my tongue to hold.

For instead of stars, planets and the sky
churning along a brittle ridge,
there are bundles of small dark irises.

Ahead of us, the sense of something smouldering,
knowing only intense observation would shoulder.

Portrait Of An Evacuee Dress

We can only imagine the day.

The cloth was purchased.
Overhead a blackening sky,
dead tired of being black leaded.
Clouds simply useless at beating back,
formations of metal droning.

Can only imagine,
the voyage overseas.
How the length
of rust colour held fast
inside the slats of a crate,
handfuls of salt air spotting.

What we know for sure
is that this hand blocked cloth,
baptised *Little Flower,*
started life as a length
of balloon cotton in rust.

We can detail
the measurements,
chart the repeat,
ninety three millimetres high
by seventy millimetres wide
and the dress height
one thousand and thirty
millimetres by seven hundred
and ninety millimetres wide.

Out of a length
came a short-sleeved
summer dress with a V-neck,
pleated front yoke,
fastened by a side zip,

two poppers
on the left shoulder,
with a waist tie that like -

Three Blind Mice,
Three Blind Mice

- had to be chased.

Printed Stuffs And Suggia's Dress

The room was Rococo, though not forbidding.

It was during this time, after working hours, side by side in silence,
me heady from printing stuff, you stiffened with madder red dressmaking
                                                            for Suggia,

that in a split second, when our heads rose from our hands,
                                                swayed from side to side

like wooden cotton reels plopped inside the bowl of a lily pond,

we each looked over each other's work, reflecting, not inspecting,

because we were wise enough to know, how light can wade, dim the eye,
depending on the strike of the hour, sudden split-pea shower.

Madame Guilhermina Suggia (1885 - 1950) was the celebrated Portuguese cello soloist painted many times by Augustus John. Toward the end of 1917 Phyllis Barron exhibited with Noel Gifford in the drawing room of Boris Antreps. Phyllis printed and Noel made the dress which Suggia wore in one of John's most admired portraits. Phyllis later went on to describe it as my first 'one-man textile show.'

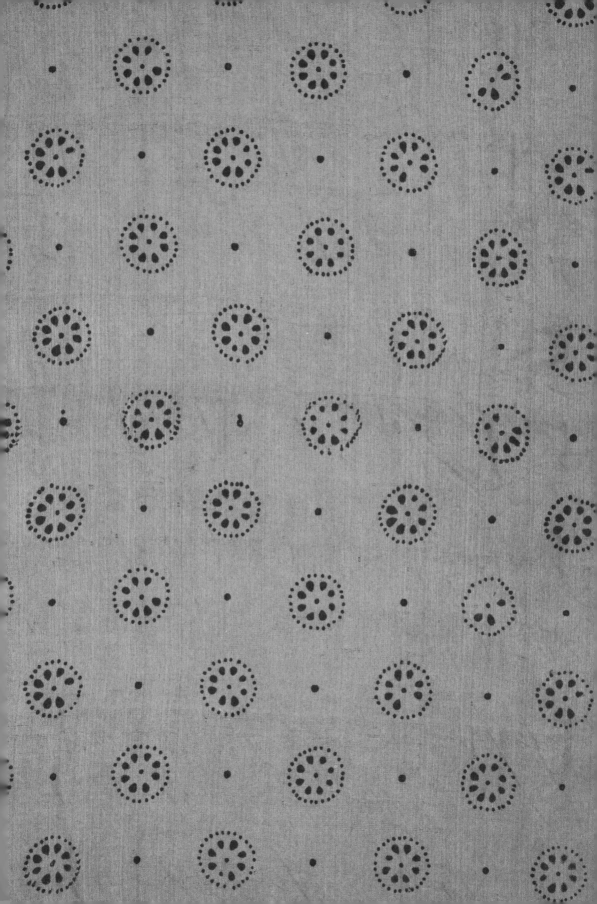

Girton Curtains

'…in our opinion, be of real and lasting aesthetic value !'

                        Phyllis Barron letter, 1932

Walking in on the room
everything glows;
old gold as lovers' bodies do in aftermath.
There, an oak dining table
tenderly nudges a chair.
By the wall, a walnut
occasional supports
a large flower glass
as air gasps at a cut single stem,
provoking pantaloons
of luminous white petals to fall.

On the polished floor
a Khelim rug wiggles
and stretches,
lounges like a Rossetti cat
in the hearth light,
whilst overhead
a pierced vellum shade
swings
and trembles,
swings
and trembles,
circled by dust motes.

Stood before the curtains,
draped and poised,
you find yourself lingering
on the twinning
of balance and harmony,
fondling with your hand
the plummets and swing.

Of course, you were right
about the need for neutral blinds -
dark string -
to prevent fading.

What was it you said?
..must not colour the light in the room,
not in any way.
For it's enough to stoke
the geometric
battlements of *Winchester*
or the mighty quills of *Little Feather*.

Step back,
watch it thrust across the back
of hard wearing linen.
The curtains pulled to and fro
sweep me off my feet -
hold high the room,
the way you would a sheaf of wheat.

Girton College Cambridge commissioned Phyllis Barron and Dorothy Larcher to design and make curtains for the Senior Common Room in 1932 - 1934. They were also approached by Fellows to advise on all areas of the new buildings, such as the Fellows Dining Room and Combination Room. Phyllis Barron and Dorothy Larcher not only designed the curtains but also proposed that the furniture should be made by the Cotswold craftsmen working in the Gimson and Barnsley tradition using excellent workmanship and design. Subsequently Frank Gardiner and Eric Sharp were employed to make the furniture. Barron and Larcher oversaw the eventual completion of the room. The designs used for the rooms were 'Winchester' for the Dining Room, and an adaptation of 'Little Feather' for the Combination Room.

Cushions For Coco Chanel

Imagine them meeting.
A salon in Paris,
long faced French windows.
Outside a balcony of wrought iron,
the design conceived
by walking at midnight through tulips.
Or if we were fanciful
place them on a yacht,
cocktails clinking, cherries gloating
through the frosted triangles of raised glasses,
while the sun in centimetres,
dilates burnt orange, rag-rug pinks.

At last we have them.
Placed on a cake-tier terrace,
with palm prints. The sky a lapel,
pinned with Bakelite
cicadas and geckos,
and their conversations
like ink drops,
being dropped, drop after drop,
from a syringe into water,
until it becomes a trail,
then dissolves,
and we can no longer follow.
Still we lie in bed thinking
and we can speculate,
like a biographer, what might
or might not have been done or said…

Do they butter each other up?
Of course, when there's prestige and money.
Yet there's mutual admiration,
though what was said is somehow,
like the finest duck feathers set aside
for the inside
of a set of commissioned cushions,
is somehow,
when the cotton liner's stuffed
and sewn, is somehow lost forever.

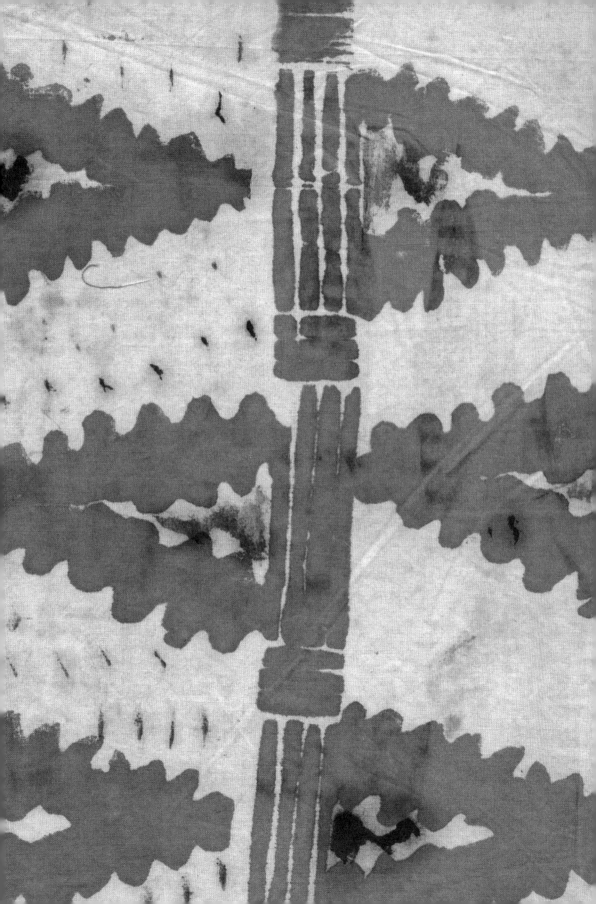

Coco Asks, *Could You Print Ankle Bracelets On Woollen Stockings?*

I could print ankle bracelets.
Yes, I'll try.
Thinking -
about how tricky
wool is when it's printed on,
always a mess,
a bloody nightmare to handle.

And by the way -
Madame angled her head -
she wouldn't settle for
just the appearance
of a cheap chain,
half-forged links,
a tart's heart clasped
and rusty-padlocked.

No, it must be something
that everyone
would instantly
recognise as Style.
That's what's required,
as she pointed out.
(And I kept it in mind
all the time in the workshop
as I drummed it out)

As she pointed out,
with her perfect leg -
using her own calf
poised and pulsating
like a Parker ink nib,
dripping squid
on the neutral carpet -
her's was the perfect calf,
her's the perfect carpet.

I distinctly remember
the smell of her breath,
not Parma violet,
more like damp indigo
when it hits the iron.

How at all times I was
to discipline
and not let the fibres bleed,
her ringmaster voice
zinging through the lash -
on points - on points,
sophistication and clarity,
and again
sophistication and clarity,
or I'd be wasting her time.

Coco Chanel (1883 - 1971) was the pioneering French fashion designer. Phyllis Barron was introduced to her and the Duke of Westminster, with whom she was living. After seeing the stuffs Coco Chanel asked if Phyllis could print bracelets onto the ankles of woollen stockings, which Phyllis tried, but failed to do. Chanel also commissioned her to make cushions for a folding mattress for a day bed or garden seat, using her hand block printed designs, for her Paris apartment. She gave specific and detailed instructions as to how they were to be made. The print is known as 'Chanel' of which only a fragment remains.

The Duke Of Westminster's Boar

The Duke relished boar hunting
but curiously kept a tame boar in a willow pen.

I say curiously: though I enjoy the look
and texture of French bread.
Yet I feed it to his boar,
and not just because I'm fascinated
by the stump work of the creature, which I am.
No. It's much more.

As the baguette's munched in his jaw,
I'm busy memorising - the way you would
a lyric - the way of the crumbs on the straw.

For *Flying Cloud* We Thought Large Or Old Captain

Horrified, we strived around the clock,
all the while pretending not to worry
about the deadline, whether the prints
would work or not, mithering about
the block's paste fast tracking into leprosy.

All the while pretending not to worry
about the deadline.
Whether the prints would work,
that is - as a flat pattern repeat
when it's applied
to a three dimensional form,
which in this instance is upholstery
such as chair seats,
or the drop - plus shrinkage -
from the cabin doors, windows.

It's like trying to compare motion
with the stillness of a dry dock.
Intriguing, but difficult
because each piece won't necessarily
make its peace with the other,
even though
it's blood sister - blood brother.

The Flying Cloud was the luxurious forty cabin yacht of the Duke of Westminster. Barron and Larcher were commissioned to design and block print fabric that could be used to furnish the interior. The interior was designed by the architect Detmar Blow. Barron and Larcher were assisted in their work by the young artist and textile designer Enid Marx.

Marx

'they broke me in'
              Enid Marx

I peer through a diamond window.
The sight of steam, petty jealousies
of mordants pressing, village women
sorting husks for dye-stuffs.
Phyllis and Dorothy are inside,
one diligently following a template,
cutting a block from battleship lino,
the other hypnotic by the sink,
washing chalk out of velvet.

I'm in there too, wrestling
a hose like an anaconda,
dreaming of the bark cloths
of Polynesia, of Africa, of New Zealand
and Persian pottery and Folk art,
of Mr Punch and Lord and Lady Clapham,
of found objects on the London street,
of light airy materials
such as organdie and balloon cotton,
leftovers of industrial production.

Home in. I have a look on my face
that's hard to disguise,
of felted rain clouds mustering,
just itching to pelt down rain,
Cornnucopia, Jeaux, Foot, Chip, Wangle,
with an overprint of black stars.
A rigmarole of stars and spots,
repeated with so much intensity
I have to laugh.

For *Sea* I see a galled iron print,
that reminds me so much of Nash,
his influences.
Underground in iron rust,
Woolworth from found,
or may'be *Wangle* again,
two colours on dyed cotton ground,
pantomime of *Richardson, Richardson* -
my hands shaking
as I rush to get it all down.

Enid Marx (1902 - 1998) textile designer, trained as an artist at The Royal College of Art, but failed her diploma in painting because her work was considered too abstract. She worked with Barron and Larcher for about a year. It was under such tutelage that she learnt the processes involved in dyeing and hand block printing. She went on to become one of the most formative textile pattern designers of the twentieth century, not only printing her own textiles but also designing for the London Underground, as well as papers for Curwen Press, which she executed from her own wood engravings.

Painswick Dandelions

I

Upstairs and well lit
stands the dye house,
converted from a cowshed.
Ahead, the long open refectory
road of battered print tables.

The beasts have long gone,
Yet there lingers a smell
of ageing Cheddar, of lint
stiffened with mould,
of hay coddled by chequered hides.

Over our heads was heaven.
A railway, the sort of thing
garage doors would run upon,
though we substituted
garage doors for star frames.
Visualise, a blue whale, mouth open -
then you have our indigo vats.

II

Sisters, you have come this far
so take a stick stool and watch,
for we have been well tutored,
we women of the village.

Underneath a naked bulb
we walk the block,
holding our heads high like a llama,
firm and steady,
strike deftly with a maul or hammer,
replace to repeat the pattern,
more of the same
and again, again, again:
a must or else the dye stuff creeps.

Cutting across wide-open plains,
sisters, we strew as Mormons,
a million sunflowers blazing.

Phyllis Barron and Dorothy Larcher trained and employed women from Painswick in their home and workshop, to help with hand block printing, sewing and finishing of the cloth. These women were Peggy Burt, Daisy Ryland, and Emily Edsall.

Mahogany Boat Seats With Infinite Possibilities

I stripped the seating grain,
the way you would makeup from a face.
I cut and gouged and stamped all day,
printing on damask, on velvet;
but the print on damask shuddered,
on velvet deformed,
so was put in a bag
out the back for the rag man.

On second thoughts,
brought back inside,
and all because the dance of light
got me thinking,
what won't work in rust
might work - after all -
with yellow in flight
as an overprint.

In The French Alps, Phyllis Eats A Marmot

The marmot
has many names,
there's the usual Latin stuff,
though I prefer
the Prairie dog,
the Alpine mouse etc.

On the terrace,
overlooking Mont Blanc,
I'll tell you how it tasted.
How its torso sank sweet
between my teeth,
tender, lounging on my tongue.

Fragrant as white wine,
disturbing,
something herbal -
berries, lichens, mosses,
roots and flowers,
around its incisors and jaw
traces of alpine whistles.

In remembrance
I'll print in velvet,
a jacket, a stole,
and perhaps,
now days are dissolving,
the lining of a phantom opera coat.

When someone asks
for a reference in the catalogue,
the autograph of the print,
I'll say with authority -
No name,
because like Kipling's Cat,
this creature walks alone.

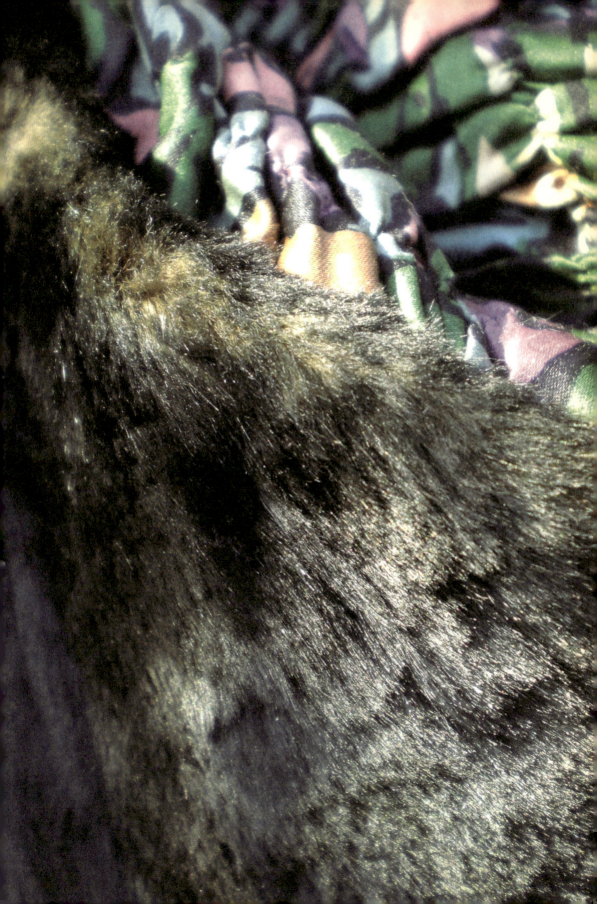

Phyllis Barron's Hat

Isn't that Phyllis Barron's hat?
You know, the one she was wearing
stood by Dorothy in the photograph.
You have to hand it to them!
What a double act, hunting
in a teeming French market.

Above the auction room skylight,
a glut of damson clouds,
steady small change of rain,
growing voice of the auctioneer,
warning, to those of us not staying,
of time left
if intent on placing commission bids.

By now, to all but the expert eye
I was casually frisking the upholstery
on the back of an Edwardian nursing chair.
You were being very, very tender
with a studio salt pig, stuck fast
between a lion honey pot and Tyneside dish.

Dyes Racing

I'd always admired that painting
by Paolo Uccello, *The Hunt In The Forest*.
Tempera and oil on panel,
I'd always envied gazehounds leaping,
twirling, dripping like honey from a honey stick,
some certain, others dithering.
It reminds me of darker dyes running
from spring water,
out of darkness before mordant.

Pastry Cutter

And this, you say, is the original pastry cutter.
And for a second I'm transported,
to that famous auction, *Elizabeth David's Kitchen,*
when fans paid a fortune for a humble table,
cracked pudding bowls, well worn wooden spoons,
and I might have mounted a cream ware cow
and jumped over the moon, if I'd been there.
But alas I wasn't born, and all this stuff - I read about.

But this is real; the table, the sample of cloth,
the length got out specially in Manchester.
A pastry cutter, block sprinting a length of cloth,
a layperson would call the colours mustard and black - a layperson.
And there are loads of examples in loads of other shades,
so beloved by the loaded, and now not-so-privileged.

But for the two of them, over in the workshop,
it was more about the effect of edges when distressed,
which one with the other worked, walked a length best,
than today, and what it might be worth on the open market.

There Was A Cloth, Sadly Now Lost, And We Called It Scaffold

I

The window looks out into a neighbour's yard
which angles, as do all the houses inside the gorge.
Terrace gardens, leering buddleia, crouches of alpines,
all the greys of lavender, mulberry, spindle berry, silver sage.
Two to three blue tits dab a bit, dab a bit more on knuckle clamps.

(If you can imagine, tit bits of yellow, tit bits of blue)

The design reflects the vertical and horizontal.
Imagine chopsticks, threaded through hair.
We printed fourteen floor-to-ceiling lengths
on furnishing weight, the finest Lisburn linen.
Think of our poor fingers we near wore to the bone.

II

After finishing the final lengths
we hung *Scaffold* to dry in a tinderbox room,
watched as it wafted from the tongue and groove ceiling,
amongst hooks of herbs and vicious teasels.

We leaned back and listened to night chaffing,
the red-backed door,
the red-backed door we think if flipped
would make a useful kitchen table.

The cloth transfixed by so many blue tits
wonders whether any of its natural state
is showing, and if not is it too late?

We take no notice. See how the dye brims to the edge
of the bird's wing, like a child's water colour.
How fast the blue to the yellow to the black curve is drying.

Gathering Home Grown Flowers From Our Painswick Garden

Stage lit by the sun, I stand
at the southern edge of our flowerbed.
Day lilies crane beside ruddy brick
as flights of dragon flies overprint.
I stoop, cut trails of indigo clematis,
blackcurrant pansies, an array
of Agamemnon old gold
polyanthus for you to paint.

I look back, is that your shadow by the bay
where the room suddenly darkens,
or your bearded yellow iris shawl
over shoulders falling,
as you walk away. It must be seconds ago
you were there, I'm sure, arranging
in a Leach studio pot something
unheard of - to doze.

Today, your name seems permanent,
resistant to what makes bleed or fuzz.
I balance each letter between each taken breath:
with every step I'm stashing colours,
with every stem I pick and loop and thread,
with every every tendril torn, every flower head,
wasp hollowed, bee begged, I'll cling.

There, In An Ercol Bottom Drawer
after Barron and Larcher

I remember all my early prints, all my experiments, my failures,
my amputees, the gougeing and scoring, scars and dents.

I printed
the excavations of an earthworm, hedgehog and mole in ointment pink
                                                                         and cutch brown.

I printed
in half-shapes, a rook, a raven, an albino crow onto fleeing indigo.

I printed
reindeer, monk jack and roe floating over a copper beech and holly hedge.

I printed pheasant, alternated with wild mallard and winter white mountain
                                                                                                           hare.

I printed
the insides of Bramley apple windfalls, sculpted by a squad of blackbirds,
                                                                                                       brown rats.

I printed
the cast of *My Antonia* in minute detail.

I printed
as a sample Lena Lingard sat sewing with Tiny Soderberg.

I printed
Christina's poem, *In an Artist's Studio*, repeatedly. First in lilac, then in purple -
                                                                                as an afterthought in black.

I printed
on silk, that last line, *Not as she is, but as she fills his dream.*

I printed,
repeatedly as an overprint, to see what might happen,
                                      what might become of the line under stress.

I printed,
what happens when a word is broken off, hung, drawn and quartered.

I printed
Not as she is, but as she fills his dream, because I couldn't stop myself.

I printed the word,
SingSong, stood back, watched as the word faded and I struggled to read.

I printed
I'll give you something to scrike about my lady, but don't know why or where it
                                                                                  came from.

I printed all of Mew.

I printed
Mondrian's dead flowers, especially his shrivelled chrysanthemums
                                      because, as an emotion, they're so little known.

I printed
Girl as a self-portrait devouring a coconut macaroon whilst holding a Celia
                                                                                                            Birtwell bag.

I printed
a version of *Every Day Authentic Dress Of The Renaissance*.

I printed
the tale of Perkins's Pink and Hoffman's Violet, under duress.

I printed, after a down pour,
the stigmata of ten rusty nails left out on the honey coloured flags.

I printed
a tongue and groove table that doubled as a chair on Kitchener Street.

I printed
a fuzzy felt zoo and a fuzzy felt farm.

I printed terns snipping the Lagan, in the style of Lucienne Day.

I printed -
with details of Demelza - all episodes of *Poldark* for the women in my family.

I printed
Jolyon and Helene from *The Forsyte Saga*.

Inside my head I have ledgers of prints, which - I have been told -
is very ambitious.

I printed
Very Very Ambitious.

I printed
tons of white flower heads, which are not cold, but a highlight.

I printed -
face to face - figures from *South Riding*. Minutes from a public meeting.

I will print the socks I saw in a case,
one with the profile of Churchill
the other the profile of Hitler,
simply because they're knitted - and it'd be fun.

I printed
a fat French hen sitting in a tin bath, as a clear narrative - not an abstract.

I experimented,
printed Hannah working her way through the family mini-bar,
with emphasis on Vodka.

I printed
Matt walking ferrets on leather leads. Matt with his rare breeds.
Matt feeding his oatmeal Icelandic ewe.

I printed
my Mum and Dad in Sardinia, in Rome, in Sicily, in Ravenna -
not as they are now, but in the 50's, early 60's.

I printed
my Aunt reading *A Time in Rome*, wearing a lemon Claire McCardle dress.

I printed
Luca and Gino with a chocolate Springer called Totti tracking
                                         through the mists for wild boar and truffles.

I printed
Where have you gone Robert McLiam Wilson? Twice - before I quit.

I printed
the birth of chocolate mousse, of lemon curd, of figs stuffed with amoretti.

I printed
Stracotto with Porcini, Zucchini, Fagiano alla Creta, Riccarelli.

I printed
my Gran unwrapping a slab of Echo for her cherry cake.

I printed
the nun gliding in *Villette*.

I printed
Joe Calzaghe's reach.

I printed
the best side of George Eliot onto alizarin.

I printed
Katherine's *Sun and Moon*, Neil's *Night In Tunisia* - eight lengths of each.

I printed
Mr Gentleman.

I remember walking a billion miles or more before the patterns translate.

Appendix

Permissions to reproduce the images and pictures appearing in this book have been granted by the following organisations and individuals who are acknowledged as the copyright holders and are detailed below. The specific names of the textile patterns reproduced in this book are as detailed in the Contents along with other images used.

Crafts Study Centre, University for the Creative Arts at Farnham:
pp:5,13,15,17,19,21,23,26,33,35,39,41,43,45,49,51,52,57,61,63,65,66,
69,71,73,81,
84,87,89,90,93,101,102,105,107,118,123

The Textiles Collection, University College for the Creative Arts at Farnham:
pp: 6,9,25

The Textiles Collection at The Whitworth Art Gallery, Manchester:
pp: 78,83,111

IPC Media: p97

Luminous compass dial on the upper wing of a Bristol F2B Fighter, property of The Shuttleworth Collection, Old Warden Aerodrome, Nr. Biggleswade, Bedfordshire. Image
provided from the private collection of John Benjamin:
p: 47

James Weir:
p: 95

Jane Weir:
pp:3,11,31,59,75,77,98,109,113,115,117

ORDER

The Little Gallery 3 Ellis S
Aug. 15 193

To M.... Barron & Miss Larcher
for Lanfranchi Inc.
Palm Beach

Please Supply the undermentioned Goods:—
(An Invoice or Delivery Note with above Order Number must Accompany the Goods)

---

1 yd Org. Large Regent Scarlet J B print
on dirty Pink ground. Pattern of
ground enclosed.

1 yd Org. 'Carte (as printed)

1 yd linen Kit & Miss - Brown BB on
T.S.

1 yd Basket UGI on OB or TS

1 yd Robson. Yellow & blue grey.
Pattern enclosed.